HOME STAGING

A Seller's Guide To Staging Their Home

Christina Serrano

Home Staging: A Seller's Guide to Staging Their Home

Copyright © 2019 By Christina Serrano

All rights reserved.

Published by Serrano Design Services

No part of this publication or any portion thereof may be reproduced, distributed or transmitted in any form or by any means, including photocopying, recording, scanning, electronic or mechanical methods, or otherwise, except as permitted under Section 107 or 108 of the 1976 United States Copyright Act, without prior written permission from the author.

ISBN-13: 978-0-578-57385-4

First Edition September 2019

Printed in the United States of America by Lulu Press, Inc.

Lulu Press, Inc.
627 Davis Drive, Suite 300
Morrisville, NC 27560
https://www.lulu.com/

Book design by Katelyn Serrano

Photo Credits
Christina Serrano: pages 1, 2, 4, 5, 15-17, 20, 25-26, 31, 36-37, 45-46, 48-49, 53
Jennifer Bowen Photography: page 57

Table of Contents

How to Stage Your Home p.1

Interior Rooms p.3

Interior Checklist p.8

Evaluation Sheet p.9

Interior Shopping List p.12

Staging Supply List p.13

Exterior Staging p.14

Exterior Checklist p.18

Exterior Shopping List p.19

Painting p.21

Painting Checklist p.28

Painting Supplies Checklist p.29

Contractors p.30

Contractor Checklist p.37

Lighting p.39

Lighting Checklist p.47

Photographing Interiors p.48

Resources p.55

Acknowledgments p.56

About the Author p.57

HOW TO STAGE YOUR HOME

Staging your home is like being the author of a book. You are creating a story about the home using its architectural bones, character and best attributes to sell it to prospective buyers. Just like setting the stage for a drama or a play, it is important to set the tone of your home. Why make such a fuss? According to www.forbes.com you only have 7 seconds to make a great first impression.

In *Home Staging: A Seller's Guide To Staging Their Home,* I've created an easy to follow series of guides to help you access the information you'll need quickly. Each guide comes with simple step-by-step instructions to help you get your home ready for market. It begins with a section on how to stage your home's interior and exterior spaces, followed by additional helpful information on paint, lighting, working with contractors, and photographing your home. At the end of each section or guide, you'll find handy checklists to keep you on track, pages for evaluation, notes, shopping and supply lists where applicable. According to the Real Estate Staging Association, staged homes usually sell on average 73% faster than non-staged homes. These same homes often sell with multiple offers and above asking price. Though there are never any guarantees, the investment of your time and money could prove to be well worth it. With all this information at your fingertips, you are sure to create a successful staging plan and enhance the value of your home!

A Step by Step Guide to Your

INTERIOR ROOMS

HOW TO STAGE YOUR HOME
Interior Rooms

1. Evaluate

The first step is to evaluate your interior and exterior spaces to see what is working and what you have that can be used for staging. You'll want to keep the key pieces that make up a room. For example, in the dining room you'll need a table and chairs. In the living room you'll want a sofa, maybe some side tables and a coffee table to create a conversational seating area. Make yourself a to-do list for each room/space. Decide what to keep or what to remove and make note of it. Sometimes it can help to take photographs of each room or space to help you see what isn't working. If you really want to be efficient you can measure each room, create your floor plan plus space plans to optimize furniture layout and traffic flow (see end of section).

2. Plumbing

Next, walk through the house to check all the appliances and plumbing. Make sure you don't have any leaking faucets or moldy caulking. Buyer's may check and inspect to make sure nothing needs fixing. You'll save yourself some time by addressing these items in advance. If you do find something, add it to your to-do list. Don't forget to purchase any necessary supplies if you're fixing things yourself.

3. De-clutter, De-personalize & Pack

In your evaluation you'll also want to take note of any piles of clutter, excess accessories (like extra small items or family photos), any extra non-functioning furniture pieces or small art pieces that aren't necessary for staging. For example, maybe you have a family room or dining room that has multiple curio cabinets in it. You'll want to remove one or all of the extra cabinets if they are cluttering your room or traffic flow. You'll only want to keep key pieces that will be used in the final design plan. All the other items can be packed up and removed for storing.

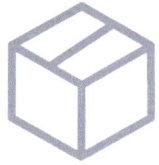

4. Traffic Flow

You'll also want to go through your home like a prospective buyer would and pay attention to traffic flow. All walkways should be open and unblocked by unnecessary furniture or items making it difficult to get through the spaces. For example, a client of mine had two sofas in a family room. The sofas were so large they actually blocked the flow of traffic into the next room making it difficult to pass by. We decided it was necessary to remove one of the sofas to make the space feel bigger and optimize their walkway.

Tip: You always want to have 36" of space for walkways and traffic flow. A prospective buyer should always be able to easily identify where to go and glide through your home. In addition, your rooms/spaces will feel larger and more open.

5 | Paint

When it comes to your home's paint, you don't want to have any dirty, chipping or peeling paint. Your home will be much more appealing to a potential buyer if it has a fresh, clean paint job. It might require a little extra work on your part and expense, but well worth the money in a great first impression. If money is a concern, concentrate on the main living spaces and the entry. In addition, it will be much easier to paint your rooms after you've uncluttered and have fewer items in your way. Try to eliminate any scuffed baseboards or molding. Touching up these sometimes forgotten areas will make your rooms shine.

Tip: Avoid dark paint colors when staging. Buyers like light colors and want to be able to see your space. With the main spaces neutral you can add pops of color with accessories to add warmth.

6 | Flooring

If your flooring is dirty or old like stained carpet or cracked tiles etc., you may want to invest in some new flooring. The few thousand dollars you spend upfront may pay you back in a much higher sales price and a faster sale. If you do decide to make this investment, you might also seek the advice of an interior designer. The designer not only will know the latest design trends, but can make sure you get the correct color tones and optimal paint/flooring selections.

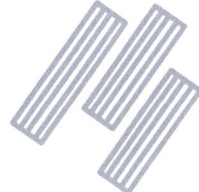

7 | Cleaning

The next step is to give the rooms a good cleaning. Make sure to mop and vacuum all flooring. You'll also need to wipe off any door handles, doors, millwork, cabinets, counters, walls, mirrors, windows, tabletops, etc. for dust, dirt, smudges or spills. Be sure that the fixtures in each bathroom are cleaned like your faucets, sinks, toilets, showers etc. Keep in mind that most potential buyers will also be inspecting these spaces and most likely look in your closets or cupboards. Another key area to check is your furniture. No stained or dirty sofas please! If you do have older furniture, perhaps consider a slipcover or get the pieces steam cleaned. I can't stress enough how important it is to have items fresh and clean. Nothing turns a buyer off like dirt, stains, and unpleasant odors!

HOW TO STAGE YOUR HOME
Interior Rooms

8 | Accessorize

Now that your rooms are freshly painted, floors cleaned and main furniture pieces are in place, it is time to accessorize the space. You might want to hire an interior designer or staging company to do this for you. The designer will make a space plan for optimum furniture placement, make sure you have correct lighting, and bring in accessories for maximum impact and balance. If you don't have the budget for a designer and are doing things on your own, the following are additional items that you'll need to consider.

Window Treatments

When addressing windows in the main areas of the home, you may need to hang curtain panels to add height to your room or remove some to let light in. Adding window treatments is also an inexpensive way to add pattern to the room. Just make sure you hang the curtains as close to the crown molding as possible. You'll also want to make sure that your panels are hung a minimum of 3" past the window frame. The main goal of the windows is to let in maximum light making your space feel as big as possible and to accentuate your ceiling height.

Art

Make sure to have balanced and proportioned artwork where needed; such as over a bed, sofa or buffet. You don't want pieces that are too small, unless you create a large grouping of items to fill the proper amount of wall space. It is always better to go with bigger pieces when in doubt. You'll also want to pay attention to subject, color, or frame and pick pieces that will enhance your design. One of the most common mistakes I've seen is a client's art hung way too high. Artwork should be hung at eye level at about 60" up from the floor. The exception to this is above a sofa or buffet. Hang your art 8" to 10" above the bottom of the furniture below it. When hanging art in situations where people might be sitting, the art should always be hung lower. If you have a wide piece like a sofa, you might need 2 or 3 large pictures or 1 very large piece to be in proportion to the furniture piece.

Lighting

You'll also really want to make sure that you have a minimum of 3 light sources in each room to ensure they are well lit. You should double check the light bulbs in your lamps and make sure they work. Light bulbs come in different color temperatures, warm, neutral and cool. Your space will look better if the color temperature of your bulbs are all the same and are a color that enhances the wall colors in your home. It is also good to have all three types of lighting: task, ambient, and accent to create good ambiance in your space. (see the Lighting Guide.)

Setting the Table

Setting the dining table like you are expecting guests for dinner is also a great idea. This not only looks nice on the table, but adds a welcoming feeling to buyers as they walk through your home. It helps them imagine how it might feel to dine in the room should they buy it. You might need to add place mats, a table runner, napkins, dishes and of course a centerpiece of some kind. Try and add texture with these items, by keeping things in neutral colors everything will mix and match well.

Linens

Along with setting the table, be sure and purchase some fresh new linens. A plush new set of bathroom towels, kitchen towels and area rugs will help these areas look much better. You might also put a basket of washcloths with a bowl of soaps in the bathroom on the counter. Adding a plant like an orchid or something simple will add warmth to these generally cooler spaces. You want to keep the counters as clear as possible.

Pillows & Throw Blankets

In rooms like the living rooms, and bedrooms you'll want to make sure you have lots of pillows on the sofa and a well-made bed. A few blanket throws here also adds comfort and texture to these spaces. A grouping of different patterned pillows makes a room feel cozy especially if they coordinate with your window treatments and furnishings. When in doubt stick with neutrals to keep things simple.

Collections

At this point in the accessorizing you can add your edited collections where needed to help accessorize your bookshelves or tabletops. When using collections in your staging keep it to items that are the same material or color. This might be a collection of white pitchers, or leather bound books that you can use to enhance kitchen shelves or bookshelves. A collection of baskets can really come in handy not only to add texture to your home, but do double duty by storing necessary items. You'll want to choose items that will strengthen the overall design look. Just keep in mind it should be kept simple, it should only be added if needed and where appropriate.

Plants

Make sure each room has plants placed in a few locations to bring some life into your space. You may want to add a Ficus tree or Fiddle Leaf fern in a corner or perhaps a vase of fresh flowers on the table. You could also add a terrarium filled with succulents or a potted orchid on the coffee table. Both of these options require minimal water but add nice color and greenery to a room. Remember to remove any dried or dead plant leaves as well as any non-thriving plants. A few touches of natural elements to a room really enhances the space.

Scents

Nothing can turn a buyer off more than if your home has a funny smell. You might need to put some baking soda in any places that you feel have odors like the home gym, fridge or freezer to help keep them fresh. Baking some cookies in the oven, adding some scented candles, or potpourri to a room can add a nice smell to your home before showing. One thing to consider is nothing too strong like florals that people might be allergic too. Instead concentrate on citrus smells like pineapple, grapefruit, lemon or orange which have a fresh scent. You could also add a bowl of fruit like apples, lemons or oranges to the kitchen counter. In bathrooms, you could add a tray of soap or bath salts to add some light scent.

HOME STAGING CHECKLIST
Interior

- [ ] **Photograph-** Take pictures of your rooms; bedrooms, bathrooms, kitchen, laundry room, living room, dining room and office etc.

- [ ] **Evaluation-** Evaluate what is working in the space and make note of which furniture pieces will be staying for the staging design.

- [ ] **To-Do List-** Create a to do list for each room of your home. Add the pieces that will stay and the ones that need to be packed or stored away.

- [ ] **Inspection-** Do a plumbing and appliance check to make sure that everything is working. Fix any leaks or broken items.

- [ ] **De-clutter-** De-clutter and de-personalize by removing family photographs and small personal items not used in staging. Pack up and move to storage.

- [ ] **Walk Through-** Walk through your home like a prospective buyer. Make sure the traffic paths are obvious, unobstructed and open. 3' or 4' of open space is a good rule to follow.

- [ ] **Paint-** Touch up paint walls, and millwork as needed. If you have dark painted walls you might consider repainting to a lighter color to make spaces feel bigger and brighter.

- [ ] **Flooring-** If you have any damaged or stained flooring, replace it. The new flooring will help your home show off its best potential.

- [ ] **Clean Up-** Make sure that everything gets a good cleaning from top to bottom. Don't forget about the appliances, garages, windows, cupboards and bathroom fixtures as buyer's may inspect some of these areas.

- [ ] **Lighting-** Make sure that you have adequate lighting with three different types of lighting. Also make sure that your light bulbs and lamps are the same color temperature. A good rule of thumb is 100 watts for every 50 sq. ft.

- [ ] **Accessorize-** Add items like window treatments, plants, scented items, pillows, throws, linens and lighting to make rooms more inviting.

EVALUATION SHEET

Space/Room:

WHAT TO KEEP FOR STAGING?
Existing furniture pieces:
_____
_____
_____

WHAT NEEDS TO BE REMOVED OR PACKED AWAY?
_____
_____
_____

DOES ANYTHING NEED REPAIR?
Are any supplies needed for this?
_____
_____
_____

WHAT NEEDS TO BE CLEANED?
Are any supplies needed for this?
_____
_____
_____

DOES ANYTHING NEED PAINTING OR TOUCH UPS?
Are any supplies needed for this?
_____
_____
_____

DOES FLOORING NEED REPLACING?
Are any supplies needed for this?
_____
_____
_____

DOES THE EXTERIOR NEED ANY REPAIRS OR ITEMS REMOVED?
Are any supplies needed for this?
_____
_____
_____

IS THERE ADEQUATE LIGHTING?
Are there 3 sources of light and correct bulb temperature?
_____
_____

Extra Notes

Floor Plan: Use this page to construct floor plans for your rooms. 1 square = 1 foot

STAGING SHOPPING LIST

Interior

Window Treatments:
Curtain Panels & Rod (where needed)

Art & Wall Decor:
Buy new wall art, mirrors, and decor items for above sofas, tables, or in main focal areas.

Lighting:
Purchase needed light bulbs, shades, lamps or fixtures that need replacing or updating.

Table Setting:
Purchase napkins, napkin rings, charger plates, china plates & bowls in different textures to create a pretty table setting. A table runner or placemats can also be used to create a welcoming table with a centerpiece at the center of the table.

Rugs:
Area rugs if needed for furniture conversational areas to define the space. New kitchen rug and bath mats for the bathrooms.

Linens:
New set of kitchen towels to put out, be sure to keep these dirt free. New sets of bath towels, hand towels, and washcloths to stage the bathrooms. One for each bath. New white sheets for bedding if needed as well as bed cover and bed skirt to look fresh and clean. Bed risers to raise bed if needed.

Pillows:
A minimum of 4-5 pillows for a sofa, recommendation 2 solid and 2 patterned. 1 lumbar pillow in a different pattern that coordinates with the room. If the room has accent chairs additional single pillows here as well.

Containers:
After reviewing your to do list, purchase containers such as baskets, bowls, trays, vases or dishes needed to complete the staging design. For example, maybe you need a vase for flowers on the coffee table.

Plants:
Purchase extra plants for corners, coffee tables or other areas like an orchid in the bathroom as needed. You might also need to purchase some dried botanicals such as a wreath, or fresh flowers for a bouquet.

Scent:
Don't forget to purchase candles in a citrus scent, fresh fruit or perhaps bath salts to add scent to your home. Just make sure it is nothing too strong or floral that might be off putting.

Bedroom Pillows:
A minimum of 3 accent pillows for a the bed, recommendation 2 solid and 1 patterned. Duvet covers are a pretty option for bed covering. New fluffy pillows on a bed are very inviting.

Plant Containers:
Purchase any necessary pots for plants and liners to catch water so there aren't any spills. I like to purchase plants then place them in larger pots with a liner for easy maintenance.

Staging Supply List

Tools

Hammer & Nails

Screwdriver & Screws

Phillips

Picture Hanging Hooks

Picture Wire

Command Strips

Tin Snips

Scissors

Pencil

Blue Painter's Tape

Level

Stud Finder

Drill & Drill Bits

Tape Measure

Steamer

Double Stick Tape

Furniture Sliders

Extension Cord

Garden Sheers

Bed Risers

Other Supplies

Apron

Cleaning Gloves & Garden Gloves

Wet Wipes

Cleaning Products, Windex etc.

Toilet Paper & Paper Towels

Duster & Extra Cleaning Rags

Magic Erasers

Furniture Polish & Scratch Cover Crayons

Safety Pins

Mop, Broom & Dust Pan

Garbage Bags

Water

Foam Carpet Cleaner

Lighter for Candles

Cleaning Bucket

A Step by Step Guide to
EXTERIOR STAGING

HOW TO STAGE YOUR HOME
Exterior Staging

1 Remove Clutter

Remove any side yard or yard clutter that may be sitting around. A dump run may be all that is necessary to remove unsightly clutter piles outside. You'll especially want to remove these types of items from the main usable parts of your yard dining and entertaining spaces where possible. This will also clear the space for paint contractors, home inspectors and potential buyers later. If you don't have access to a truck, you might consider hiring a company to help with the clean up. This could save you time and be well worth the effort.

2 Paint

No chipping or peeling paint outside. If it is in the budget a fresh coat of paint on the exterior could do wonders to your curb appeal. There are many recommended paint combinations at your local paint store or you can seek advice from an interior designer here as well.

3 Remove Dead Plants & Weeds

Take a good look outside. Stand across the street of your home and see: what is working and what isn't? Make note of any weed patches or dead plants. You'll want to cut away, remove and dispose of all dead items. You may also have to prune back or reshape shrubs or trees. Keep your lawn trimmed and flower beds neatly manicured.

4 Flower Beds

Take a good look at any flower beds, maybe you need to add more plants or create better curb appeal with a repetition of the same plant in rows. For example, maybe a row of medium sized Gardenia shrubs with a smaller row of a colorful ground cover in front is all you need to give front windows a polished look. By repeating the plants you can draw the eye across the front of the house or up to the front door.

5 | Fertilize

Give your lawn or plants a good dose of fertilizer to increase their color depth and growth. Not only will your plants look better, it will encourage flower blooms so your yard looks lush and colorful.

6 | Bark

It is amazing how a fresh coat of bark can really enhance your flower beds. This is an inexpensive touch, but can really give a fresh manicured feeling to your exterior. The bark will also act as a great protective layer for your existing plants.

7 | Potted Plants

Adding some full flower pots to the porch or walkway sends an inviting message to guests as they approach your front door. If you use plants like lemon thyme or scented geranium, you'll add delicious scent as well. Be sure to pick plants that are suited for the sun's location. If your porch is sunny, you want plants that are going to be able to withstand the heat. If you aren't sure what to choose ask your local garden center. Keep it simple here and pick colors that coordinate with your flower beds and compliment your home's color.

8 | Front Door

A nicely painted front door, door mat, and seasonal wreath is also a very welcoming touch. If you want people to remove their shoes when entering your home, you might place a shoe basket somewhere close by either inside or outside. You can tie a tag on the basket with a note that says, please remove shoes.

9 | Sidewalks & Paths

Make sure all the walkways are swept, washed and clean. If you have any outside furniture, make sure the cushions are dusted and clean as well. Be sure to think of these outside seating areas like the inside and accessorize accordingly. You may need to add lanterns, cushions, plants or an umbrella as accessories to make these spaces feel welcoming.

10 | Lighting

Don't forget to check exterior lights and make sure they are all in good working condition, dusted and clean. Replace any broken or non-working fixtures or bulbs. Make sure your bulb colors match!

11 | Pools

If you have a swimming pool, make sure it is clean and extra accessories are properly stored away.

12 | Animals

If you have dogs or other outside animals be sure to have a plan in place for showings. You'll also want to make sure to clean up after them daily. This way potential buyers can walk freely around your yard.

HOME STAGING CHECKLIST

Exterior

- ☐ Remove clutter from the yard, donate old and unwanted items or dispose of.

- ☐ Paint the exterior of the home if budget allows and if needed.

- ☐ Remove any dead tree branches, dead plants or weeds to encourage new green growth. Keep lawn and border shrubs nicely manicured.

- ☐ Evaluate existing flower beds and pots to see if any new plants are needed to enhance curb appeal. When adding new plants add a group of the same variety for repetition and cohesion.

- ☐ Fertilize existing lawn and plants to promote green coloring and new growth.

- ☐ Update flower beds with bark to help protect plants and give a fresh clean look.

- ☐ Add additional potted plants to the porch or walkway as needed. Plant a taller plant in the center, fill in with a medium sized plant and edge the planter with a trailing plant so it is full and colorful.

- ☐ Make sure front door paint is in good condition, if not paint. Add a door mat and seasonal wreath for a welcoming touch.

- ☐ Sweep and wash all porches, sidewalks and paths to and around the home.

- ☐ Make sure all exterior lighting is working.

- ☐ Accessorize any outdoor seating areas with cushions, pillows, umbrellas, plants etc. as needed.

- ☐ Clean up after pets daily, and have a property showing plan for pets.

- ☐ If you own a pool, keep pool and surrounding areas clean.

STAGING SHOPPING LIST
Exterior

Flower Bed Plants

Fertilizer

Bark

Potted Plants

Wreath

Door Mat

Shoe Basket

Outside Umbrella (if needed)

Outdoor Pillows and Cushions

Outdoor Furniture (if needed)

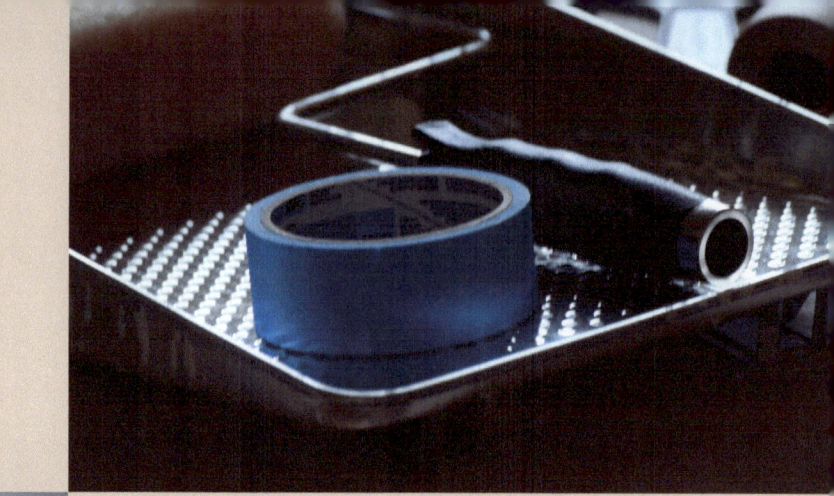

A Step by Step Guide to
PAINTING

PAINTING YOUR HOME

Nothing tells a story better than the colors found all around us each day. Color is in everything from our clothing, to our homes, and the nature that surrounds us. Color is also a very personal choice. We choose colors that make us feel good and color can affect our mood by its intensity or softness.

To help you choose colors to stage your home, I've suggested a few neutral tones at the end of this paint guide. Light shades of gray and beige work well for home staging. The following information provides you with the tools necessary to select the right paint type, sheen, and color for your project.

HOW TO STAGE YOUR HOME
Painting

1. Planning

Before you begin your painting project you'll need to evaluate your rooms or spaces and decide what type of look you want. Will you want warm or cool colors? What types of activities will be taking place in the space and are the color samples selected appropriate? Maybe you'll take inspiration from nature or a favorite painting or object. Make sure to select paint colors you love.

Tip: When selecting a color remember paint always dries darker. When you've chosen a color you like try the next shade lighter on the walls first and it should be just right. You can always go darker if you decide it isn't dark enough.

2. Different Types of Paint

There are many different options when choosing a brand of paint. A good paint store can help you select the product that will be best suited to your space. Here are a couple of things that are important to know.

Paint has different chemical compounds that can off gas a strong odor that can be unhealthy to breath. Always be sure to work in an area that is well ventilated when painting. The healthiest paint options to choose for your home are paints that contain no VOCs (volatile organic compounds) or have very low VOCs. When selecting paints you always want to use the appropriate interior or exterior selection based on the project and ones with the least VOCs.

I prefer to use the more expensive line of paints from the paint stores. The more expensive paint tends to have better coverage and will save you money in the long run because it will require fewer coats to cover an area. For example, I had a client who started a project with cheaper paint. The paint was as thin as water. Although they applied 3 or 4 coats of paint, the coverage was uneven and not to their liking. In the end the cheaper paint cost more because of the additional applications, and work required than if

they had just paid a little bit more for the better quality paint in the first place.

Tip: A good paint contractor will always apply primer to a project before the paint for better application and durability.

3 Selecting Sheen

Paint comes in many different types of sheens for different types of purposes. Higher sheen paints or gloss sheens are good for bathrooms and spaces that need washing. Lower sheen or low gloss paints are good for hiding flaws and are less reflective.

Here is a general guide:

Gloss

Gloss is very reflective, toughest finish and most stain resistant, but will highlight wall imperfections. Gloss is good for smooth finishes like cabinetry, trim and woodwork.

Semi-Gloss

This sheen is less than gloss and still has good stain resistance and coverage, and is easy to clean. It can be good in bathrooms or kitchens and also for trims and woodwork.

Satin/Eggshell

These paints are great for most areas, they have a slight sheen, but still offer good coverage and are easy to clean. Walls, trims, and most rooms look great in Eggshell/Satin sheen paints. These sheens are two of the most used today.

Low Sheen

Has a little bit more sheen than flat paint and might be good in areas that won't need to be washed as much such as hallways.

Flat Paint

Flat paint is great for walls that have lots of imperfections. It is non-reflective, however it is porous and will attract dirt. Flat paint is also not as easy to clean. Stains can be difficult to remove from flat paint.

4 | Sample Colors

Once you've selected the type of paint you want and the sheen you can select some sample colors you like for your room's walls, trims, doors etc. Make note of each color and what they are for by taking a photo with your phone or creating a digital folder for paint samples. Paint a 2' x 2' square on all the walls so you can see the how the colors look in the different types of lighting. You can also see if your paint store has peel and stick samples to try out on your walls. These are a great tool to try on some new color options to see how you might like them. To make sure you are getting the right paint color on the wall place the swatch vertically on the wall, not horizontally. This will help produce a more accurate color reading. Check the color on all sides of the room throughout the day and see how the light is reflected by the other sources of lights in the evening. Do this before committing to a color. Remember color affects our mood for example red colors excite while blue colors relax.

Tip: A good thing to remember when painting different colors next to one another is to make sure that each color is in the same hue value or the same paint color family.

5 | Calculation for Paint

1 Gallon of paint covers approximately 400 sq. ft. of surface area. This may vary depending upon the condition and color of the area to be painted. You'll want to start by getting the measurements for each wall of the space width x height and add them together. Then you can subtract any windows or doors also by width x height. Adding this all together should give you the correct calculation. So for a room that is 10' x 10' and 8' high with a 7' x 3' door and 5' x 3' window. You would have (80 + 80 + 80+ 80=320 sq. ft.) - (21' +15' or 36') for a total of 284 sq. ft. The necessary paint would be 2 gallons of paint and 1 gallon of primer for coverage of a coat of primer and two coats of wall color. If you're uncomfortable with the calculations on your own, have the paint store or your paint contractor double check your figures.

6 | Price Quotes

Get price quotes from experienced paint contractors, and be sure to check references. Make sure they are licensed, bonded, and insured. Get a detailed estimate with scope of work clearly defined and guarantees of work performed. Be sure to ask how many coats of primer and paint they will be applying. Ask for a timeline of work to be completed; paint can take anywhere from 3 days+ depending upon the amount of work that needs to be done.

7 | Final Selection

Select final colors and designate colors for walls, trims, etc. Give colors to contractor for paint ordering or purchase paint if you're painting yourself. Record your selected colors in a home journal for future reference.

8 | Supplies

With the colors selected you are ready to purchase supplies for your project. Here is a list of basic supplies: primer, paint, painter's tape, cutting brushes, paint tray and liner, handy pail and liner, roller and cover, extension pole, ladder and/or scaffolding, sponges, wet-wipes and rags for clean-up, drop cloths, plastic, and craft paper with tape for baseboards, and a bucket for clean-up.

9 | Prep Work

Prep the area to be painted, move out any items from the wall or big furniture pieces that might be in the way. Store these items in another room or space. Make sure to clean walls and surfaces. Remove any switch or electric plug covers. Patch any holes that need filling with spackling paste (I prefer the colored

HOW TO STAGE YOUR HOME
Painting

varieties so you can tell when they are dry) and sand if needed. Remember to tape any surfaces such as trim etc. and to place drop cloths down before painting. If a contractor is doing the work make sure everything is properly prepped and protected.

10 | Primer

Make sure to prime the walls before painting and follow up with two coats of paint in your finish color. To keep rollers and brushes from drying out between coats wrap or seal them in plastic bags. This way you don't have to wash them until you're all finished with your project.

11 | Touch-Ups

Once the paint has dried look back over everything for any chatter marks or spots that need touching up. If you do find marks use a small brush to fill these spots in.

12 | Clean-Up

After everything is painted make sure to remove all the tape, drop cloths etc. Return the switch and electrical covers and clean up your brushes and rollers. You may need to sweep and or mop as well. Having a bucket handy with soapy water is a great way to keep brushes from drying out with paint. If using a contractor he or she should do the necessary clean-up for you. With clean up complete and furnishings returned to the space all that is left is to enjoy your new room!

13 | Staging Paint

To choose paint for staging, choose neutral colors like BM Pale Oak, SW Agreeable Gray or KM Rotunda White or choose another color that works well with your homes interior finishes. These light colors brighten up spaces but still add warmth. You'll also want to make sure that your trim and door paint is clean and touched up if necessary.

PAINTING CHECKLIST

General

- [ ] **Planning-** Take time to think about what type of look you want in your home and what colors you want to paint.

- [ ] **Evaluate-** Evaluate your spaces to determine what type of paint you'll need and which type of sheen you will choose.

- [ ] **Color Sample Selection** -Select some color samples to try out in your space.

- [ ] **Calculations-** Calculate how much paint and primer you are going to need.

- [ ] **Get Quotes-** If you are not painting yourself get some quotes from experience paint contractors for your painting project.

- [ ] **Final Color Selection-** Finalize color selections for the project. Be sure to make note of what paint, sheen, and color for the different parts of the project for future reference.

- [ ] **Purchase Supplies-** Purchase necessary supplies, see supply list checklist as a reference. If hiring a contractor he or she should have necessary supplies.

- [ ] **Prep Work-** Complete necessary prep work to get the space ready for painting. Start by removing all furnishings from the space. Remove any switch and electrical covers as needed. Cover any items that will remain in the space while painting for protection. Clean surfaces and fill any holes with spackling as needed.

- [ ] **Primer-** Make sure to apply primer to surfaces to be painted or make sure your contractor applies primer.

- [ ] **Touch-Ups-** After painting over the primer with a few coats be sure to touch up any areas that need it or may have chatter marks.

- [ ] **Clean Up-** After everything has dried, clean up and remove all tape, plastic, and drop cloths. Return switch covers and furnishings to the space. Now you are ready begin staging or to enjoy the new room!

PAINTING CHECKLIST

Supplies

- ☐ Primer and paint.

- ☐ Painter's tape.

- ☐ Paint roller and cover with extension pole.

- ☐ Cutting brushes, small flat art brush for touch-ups and edge roller.

- ☐ Paint tray with plastic liners, have one for each color you're painting with.

- ☐ Handy pail with liners.

- ☐ Ladder and or scaffolding if needed.

- ☐ Sponges, wet wipes and rags for cleaning spills.

- ☐ Drop cloths to protect flooring.

- ☐ Plastic rolls to cover windows.

- ☐ Craft paper with tape rolls to protect baseboards.

- ☐ Bucket of soapy water for cleaning brushes.

- ☐ Spackle paste, caulking and putty knife to fill holes.

- ☐ Plastic ziplock bags to store brushes.

A Step by Step Guide to Working with
CONTRACTORS

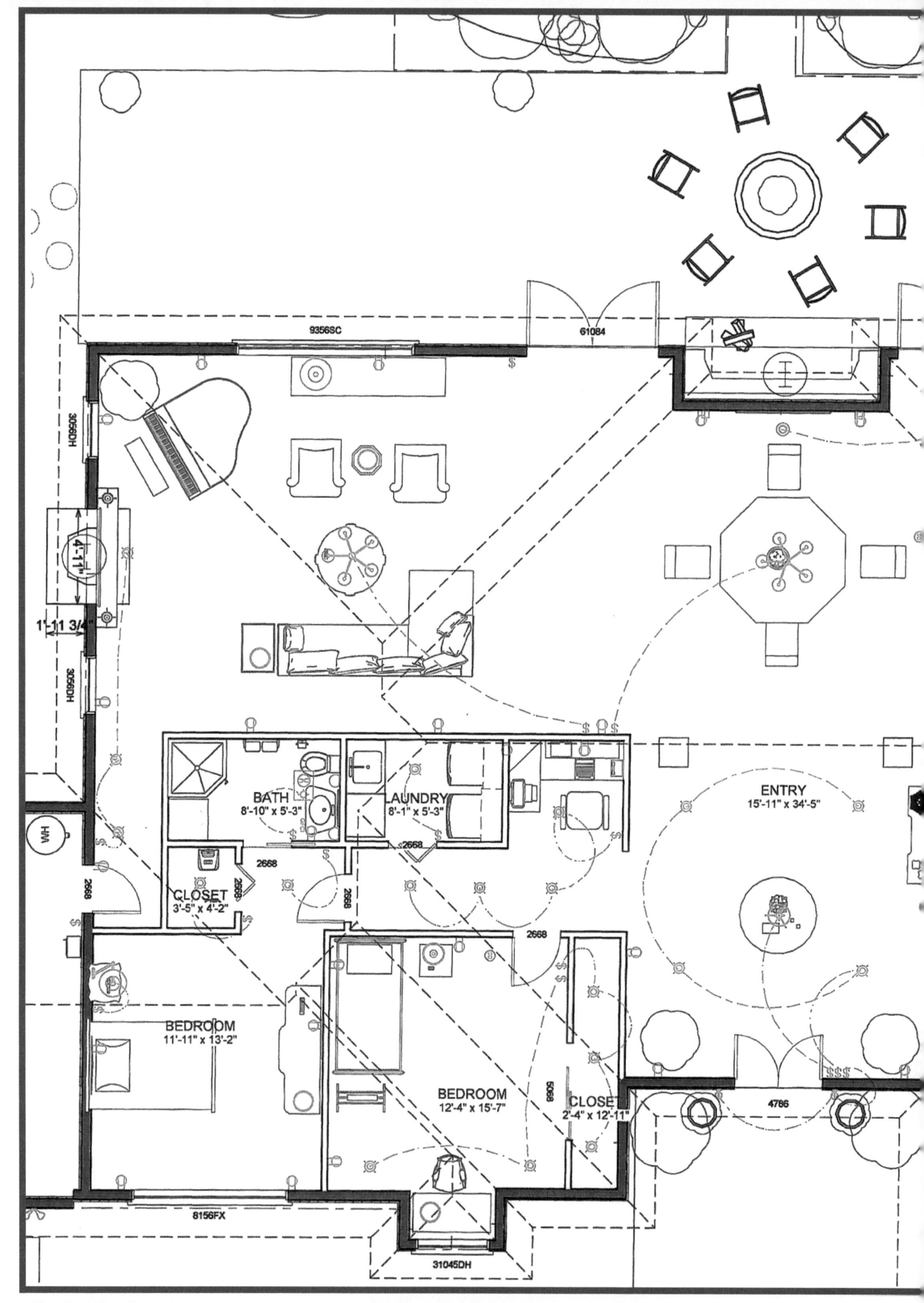

WORKING WITH CONTRACTORS

When working with contractors, here are a few of the things I find most helpful. By using the following tips, you will help make sure your project is completed on time and with no unexpected surprises or disappointments.

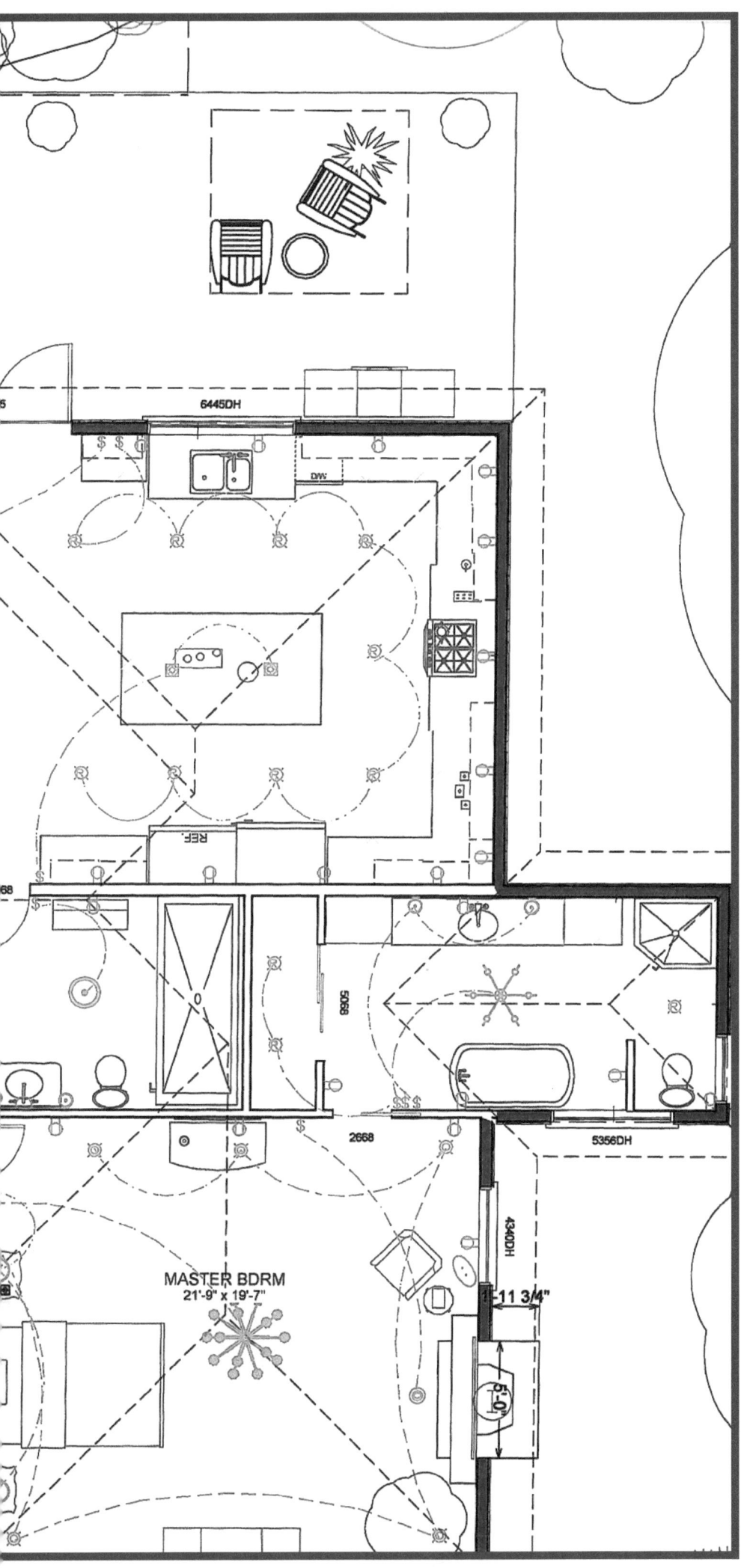

HOW TO STAGE YOUR HOME
Contractors

1. License & Insurance

It goes without saying, but make sure that the contractor has a current state license, be sure to get this number and make sure he or she is bonded and insured. Also ask to see their insurance certificate and make sure they have workman's comp and general liability coverage in case a problem arises.

2. References

Check to make sure there aren't any complaints about that license or bad reviews online. Ask for at least 4-5 references and check those out as well. Ask questions like, was the job completed on time and did they stay within the estimated budget? Did the contractor arrive on time, respect your property, and were they easy to communicate with? Did they do a good job with preparing the work site and with cleaning up? Were there any problems that came up? If so, were they resolved to your satisfaction? Would you hire them again?

3. Set the Appointment

Once you have made the call, and set up your appointment, make sure they arrive on time. Also make sure that they have good communication and respond to inquiries in a timely fashion. If they continuously arrive late or seem to lag in their communication, it could mean they are doing multiple jobs. With multiple jobs, they may not have time to give your job their full attention. Also be sure and ask up front how many jobs they will be working on while they work for you.

4. Get an Estimate

When working with contractors, get estimates in writing with a detailed list of the scope of work or repairs to be done. Also ask about their guarantees or warranty info where appropriate. This helps protect you in case there is a problem. It will provide you with a written copy to refer to. If changes are made during construction or the job, get those in writing as well. For example, if it is electrical work make sure that all parts, labor, and specific details are clearly stated on your estimate. Be wary of vague or non-specific estimates and never pay more than 33% of the job upfront. Hold back the final payment until the job is completed to your satisfaction.

5 Ask for a Timeline

Make sure to get a time frame from the contractor for how long the work will take. A good contractor should be able to provide a realistic time frame or schedule of repairs to get the required repairs done.

6 Expectations

Ask your contractor what you can do to help make his job easier. Usually, construction work is done in a specific order. Some items for repairs need to be ordered weeks in advance to keep the schedule running smoothly. Your contractor might want you to order these items first.

7 Construction Drawings

Have your floor plan and any elevation drawing copies ready to give to your contractor. This will help him or her create the look of the design you are after. This could also help save mistakes that might cost you both if something is missed.

8 Written Receipt

Finally, when all the work is complete, get a paid in full receipt. A good contractor will be more than happy to provide one for you.

9 Create a File

When you find good contractors that you are happy with be sure to keep a file or record of them for future use.

By following these tips, you'll be well prepared and protected in case a problem comes up. Working with contractors does not have to be a stressful or disappointing experience. With the proper research, communication, and expectations, you will be able to ensure the successful completion of your project.

CONTRACTOR CHECKLIST

General

- [ ] **License and Insurance-** Check to make sure your contractor has both of these and provides you with the necessary information.

- [ ] **References-** Ask for references at least 4 or 5 previous customers that you can speak with to verify satisfaction of work completed.

- [ ] **Set the Appointment-** Once verified, set the appointment.

- [ ] **Get your Estimates-** Be sure to get all estimates of work to be performed in writing and any change orders also in writing. Never pay out more than 33% deposit before the job is completed.

- [ ] **Verify Timeline-** Next, be sure to verify the timeline of how and when the work will be completed.

- [ ] **Expectations-** Discuss expectations, ask if there is anything you need to do to help keep the timeline on schedule like selecting or ordering parts.

- [ ] **Construction Drawings-** Remember to design plans or construction plans handy to avoid mistakes or confusion.

- [ ] **Receipt-** Make sure to request a written receipt with final payment for completed work. Never pay fully until the job is done to your satisfaction.

- [ ] **Future File-** Create a file for contractors that you are happy with for future work.

A Step by Step Guide to
LIGHTING

LIGHTING YOUR HOME

Lighting like color can create different feelings or a mood in our rooms. This is why it is an important element to pay attention to and it is necessary to have a plan for the lighting in your home. The different colors and amounts of light create different atmospheres. Dark spaces with poor lighting can make us sleepy and less productive. Bright spaces tend to feel welcoming, but if a room is too bright it can also be uncomfortable. Warm golden colored light feels cozy and comforting. Cooler blue lighting promotes productivity. Paying attention to the different types of light helps you create the atmosphere you want. The color and output of the light you choose should complement your personal style and taste. It should make you feel comfortable and at your best.

HOW TO STAGE YOUR HOME
Lighting

The Color of Light

When viewing anything in nature and in interiors, we find there are 3 main colors of light: warm, neutral and cool. These colors can be found on the Kelvin Color Temperature Scale. This scale was created as a guide to the different types of color that light produces. There is a color temperature or color of heat that a light source produces and emits. The hotter the light source, the cooler the temperature on the kelvin color temperature scale. The cooler the light source, the warmer the kelvin color temperature or the warmer the light is emitted from the light source. We'll look at this further when determining how to choose the correct bulb.

Lighting Sources

Additionally, there are different types of lighting sources that can be used in our homes. The first and most natural source of light that can be found in our homes is sunlight. Daylight produces the truest color of light. Daylight is the best form of light because it is a neutral colored light. Most other colors in a room or space will look their best and clearest in daylight.

After hours, in the evening or on a rainy day, we use artificial light sources. The primary artificial light sources for our homes today are lamps or light bulbs such as: incandescent, halogen, fluorescent and LEDs or (light emitting diodes). Incandescent bulbs usually produce a warmer light and give off warm light tones. Generally, fluorescent lights give off a cooler light. However with today's manufacturers you can find bulbs in both warm and cool tones depending upon their kelvin temperature. If you'll be using fluorescent bulbs, the color corrected fluorescent bulbs are best. Halogen bulbs are a kind of incandescent bulb. These bulbs emit clear white light. Halogen bulbs are the ones used to light jewelry stores making their jewelry sparkle and shine. Which type of bulb do you choose?

How to Choose a Bulb Color

Looking at daylight, we know this is the closest to neutral color on the temperature scale and will provide the best light. This is because the light doesn't cast any additional color tones. Colors are illuminated in their truest state. The goal when buying bulbs is to look for and purchase bulbs that emit neutral light or the right color of light for your home environment. The kelvin temperature of 4000 is the closest to daylight. Look for bulbs with this type of kelvin number or in the range of 2700-4000 kelvin. By choosing light bulbs that compliment furnishings, wall colors and spaces, they will look their best. Understanding the Kelvin temperature helps you select the right colored bulbs/lamps for your light fixtures.

To see how this might be relevant and important, let's look at how it applies to your home. If you have a home that has cooler

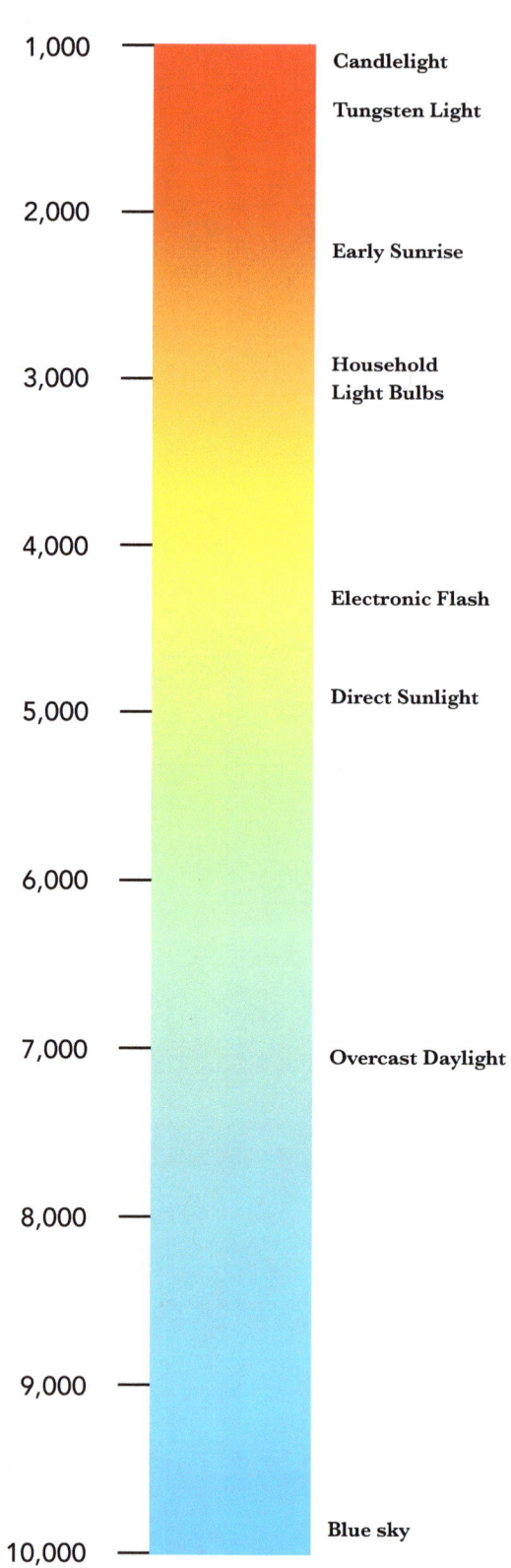

Kelvin Temperature Scale

walls in blue/gray, then it is good to get bulbs or lamps that are neutral or cooler in tone. In this case, you'll probably want a bulb that is closer to the 4000 kelvin. These bulbs would be higher on the kelvin temperature scale producing light cooler in tone complimenting the cool colored walls. Bulbs that are warmer in the 2700 kelvin range up to 3000 kelvin would be a little bit warmer than daylight. These bulbs would cast more of a warm tone or glow. These warmer temperature bulbs would compliment homes or rooms with warmer richer colors on the walls and furnishings. Your golds, yellows, oranges and reds would look better in light emitted from these warmer bulbs.

It is also very important to have your lighting be consistent throughout your home. Nothing looks more distracting when you come into a room and you see different colored lights. For example, in a kitchen maybe you look up and see a pattern of 6 recessed can lights, but each can is emitting a different color of light. It is very distracting to the eye and the eye notices that something is off. It can also cast some really funky shadows or odd colors in your space. Consistent lighting color looks much more professional and is a must! When you have bulbs that are the wrong color temperature in a room they can change fabric colors, dull your paint colors and leave a room feeling uninviting.

Today's trend in lighting is moving toward more LED lighting. New led lighting has a good CRI (Color Rendering Index). The CRI is another way to measure color and the main thing to remember is a CRI of 70-80 is good for interior residential lighting.

Bulb Output

In addition to the lamp or bulbs color you need to pay attention to its output. In the past, we looked at wattage of a bulb to decide what to select. Wattage referred to how much energy a bulb produced. Today wattage is being replaced by lumens. Lumens are the new standard and show the maximum light output. For example an old 60 watt bulb would be the equivalent of an 820 lumen bulb. Both Halogen and LED lighting are the most recommended bulbs. LED bulbs offer better energy

Lumens
(brightness)

Watts (energy)	Lumens
150 w	2600 lm
100 w	1600 lm
75 w	1100 lm
60 w	800 lm
40 w	450 lm

efficiency, a longer life span, and true color rendering. LEDs do however cost more.

Options of Lighting

Another thing that is really important is knowing there are many different sizes and styles of bulbs. Today there are a lot of options when purchasing bulbs. For example, you can get different colored bulbs, or you can get bulbs with different types of filament. Most of the time, you'll want white or clear bulbs, but there are times when you might need a different type of bulb. Let's say you have a chandelier in a dining room. This type of bright light can be hard on the eyes. You can purchase bulbs that have been spun with fabric fibers on the inside or frosted so the light is filtered producing a softer light. You could also accessorize your candle lights with shades to diffuse the light in a softer way.

Function

It is important to think about the function of your home's lighting needs. You'll need to check your fixtures to make sure you have the correct output for your fixture.

Another recommendation is to add different switches for some fixtures. By adding dimmer switches, you can manipulate and control the amount of light at different times of the day. This helps to adjust it for different tasks. To create a romantic dinner, for example, you could dim the dining room chandelier to soften the light. You could also dim the lights in a child's room for a night light.

When evaluating the function of light fixtures for our lighting needs, it is important to understand the three different types of lighting used in our interiors. These three different types of lighting are ambient, task, and accent. Every home needs a combination of all three types of lighting for successful illumination.

Ambient

First you'll need ambient or general lighting. Ambient lighting is lighting designed to fill a space like a ceiling mounted fixture in a room. General lighting spreads out to illuminate the space. Walking down a hallway, an ambient light could be recessed can lighting. In a bedroom you may find a ceiling flush mounted light.

Task

Task or local lighting is just that. Task lighting is designed to light up a space for a specific task or function. At a dining table, the task light might be a chandelier hanging over the table. This light fixture not only is designed to help you see while you eat, but it also helps to create a warm ambiance. If you are trying to read sitting in a chair, the task light might be a standing light fixture or a table lamp. The light fixtures here are designed to help you complete specific tasks.

Accent

Accent lighting is designed to highlight or illuminate an object or specific item in a room. It might be a picture lamp hung over a painting designed to show it off. You might have sconces next to a mirror in a dining room to create a mood or feeling. These little touches add a lot to spaces, especially in a home that is darker. By adding a pair of sconces in the room, you increase your light, accent your furnishings, and with dimmers applied create a softer light.

Placement

It is also important to think about placement of your light fixtures. Having the three types of light sources around your rooms, some above, some accenting certain objects, or for specific tasks, you'll have an environment that is very warm and pleasing. The goal is to bounce light all the way around the room or space to give you a great result. You'll also want to pay attention to shadows and how the light source will reflect when the lamps are turned on. For example, you might want lighting in your family room to be placed all around the room to provide full light coverage.

Guidelines

There are also general guidelines or measurements of where to locate your light fixtures. In addition, there are also formulas for correct size selection of lampshades. You'll want to consider these guidelines when selecting and installing your light fixtures and shades. Remember, every situation is different and sometimes the guideline might need adjustment. Here are a few typical guidelines by room.

Kitchen

Over a kitchen island a pendant light should be hung 36"-48" from the counter surface to the bottom of the pendant light. When installing multiple lights over an island the recommendation is to space the fixtures a min of 30" apart (side to side). If installing a long light fixture over an island choose one no more than 2/3 the length of the island. In larger sized rooms you'll

HOW TO STAGE YOUR HOME
Lighting

want to consider larger light fixtures. In a kitchen, under cabinet lighting is always recommended to highlight the backsplash area.

Living Room/Family Room

In a hallway, or living room space when installing multiple sconces you want to leave a minimum of 6' to 10' between each fixture for a balanced spread of light. You'll want to place the sconces between 55-65" off the floor. If you have a big mirror evenly space the lamp fixtures around it. When lighting a family or living room make sure you have light in each corner of the room. It is also important to have a floor lamp, sconce or table lamp by every reading chair or by each end of the sofa. When choosing sofa lamps you can have different styles, but make sure that the size, style and height of the lamps are similar for cohesion.

Bedrooms

You want to make sure you have ample light for reading when in bed. When positioning light fixtures in a bedroom beside a bed, you want to make sure that you can easily reach the fixture switch to turn it off and on. For best results you want to hang a sconce here 50"-55" up to the top of the sconce from the floor. The height here might need to be adjusted to the height of your bed. A table lamp shade should sit up 20"-22" from the table top to provide good light for reading.

Dining Room

A chandelier over a table should be 30"-36" from the bottom of fixture to the table top. These types of fixtures should be put on dimmers so the amount of light can be adjusted as needed. The light fixture should also compliment the shape of the table and be between 1/2 - 2/3 in size of the table's diameter. Another formula for measuring your light fixture for over a dining table is to divide the table width in half and look for a fixture with a diameter in that size range. So for a table that is 42" wide you'll be looking at 21" in diameter fixture.

Exterior

Additional lighting measurements to note, when mounting exterior light sconces, the fixtures should be placed close to eye level about 60"-65" up from the floor/ground and at least a quarter of the height of the door. So for an 8 foot door you'd be looking at a fixture about 24" tall. A bigger fixture always looks better than something too small.

Hang chandeliers 30"-36" up from table top & hang pendant lights about 30" apart and 36"-48" above counter top.

HOW TO STAGE YOUR HOME
Lighting

Lampshades
When choosing lamp shades, here's what you need to know.

1. You'll want to make sure the width of the shade of your lamp is at least twice the size of your lamp base. Be sure to take into consideration your table size.

2. The lampshade height should be 1/3 of the lamp base's height.

3. When seated the base of the lampshade should be at eye level usually up about 20"-22" from the table top.

4. If you're hanging bedside table sconces or lamps you'll want to make sure the base of those shades sits at about 20" above the top of your mattress. These measurements ensure you'll have ample lighting when seated in bed.

Installing
Finally, always contact an electrician to properly install light fixtures for you. Not only will the electrician get the job done quickly, but he or she can give great advice on spacing recessed fixtures and bulb placement.

Options
There are many different styles of light fixtures today from antique to contemporary and modern. Overhead lighting doesn't have to be mechanical looking or boring. For example in a big room, you may want to take out a ceiling fan and replace it with a beautiful eye catching light fixture. Updated fixtures can help give your home a more current look especially when being put on the market. Please be creative when selecting your lighting. A good lighting store like Lumens, Circa Lighting or Lamps Plus will have many options to choose from. Don't be afraid to break the rules. Who knows you might love the look of hanging an exterior lantern in the kitchen. More importantly, choose fixtures that work well with your home's design style. With the correct size and style you'll help give your home a great first impression.

Sconces hang 50"-55" from the floor 6' to 10' apart & table lamps are positioned so bottom of the shade is 20" up from table top.

LIGHTING CHECKLIST
Home

- [ ] **Evaluation-** Evaluate what lighting needs are in rooms. Make note of areas that are poorly lit and areas of exiting lighting.

- [ ] **Identify Colors-** Identify your home's light color. Do you have warm, neutral or cool tones?

- [ ] **Inspection-** What type of existing fixtures do you have and what might be missing? Make a list for each room or space.

- [ ] **Kelvin Numbers-** Select or make note of which Kelvin temperatures you'll need for your light bulbs. (Typical range 2700-4000)

- [ ] **Walk Through-** Walk through your home and double check do you have all three types of lighting, ambient, task and accent in each room?

- [ ] **Placement-** Do you have light fixtures placed all around the room?

- [ ] **Guidelines-** Remember to refer to the guidelines when selecting new fixtures and install bulbs with proper lumen output for best performance.

- [ ] **Consistency-** Make sure that the color of your lighting is consistent.

- [ ] **Installation-** If you run into trouble, don't hesitate to call the electrician to help out.

- [ ] **Options-** Don't forget that there are lots of options out there, be sure to choose fixtures you love.

A Step by Step Guide to
PHOTOGRAPHING INTERIORS

TAKING GREAT INTERIOR PHOTOGRAPHS

Taking great interior photographs is an important step to marketing your home. With your staging complete, the scene has been set and now you're ready to capture your home's best moments. Remember to pay attention to the camera frame. When you go to take your photos scan the outside of the frame and inside to make sure the view is visually the best it can be. You can always change your angle, adjust your lens, or move closer to crop to the frame you want. Be sure to take both vertical and horizontal images, and you may want to use a variety of lenses if you have them. A wide lens will capture the largest shot of a room. A zoom lens can capture some of those vignette or close-up moments. By following these and the following tips, you're sure to get some great shots for your marketing.

HOW TO STAGE YOUR HOME
Photography

Gather Your Tools

First you'll need to get your tools ready and have them packed to go for staging day. Here are the tools I usually bring with me:

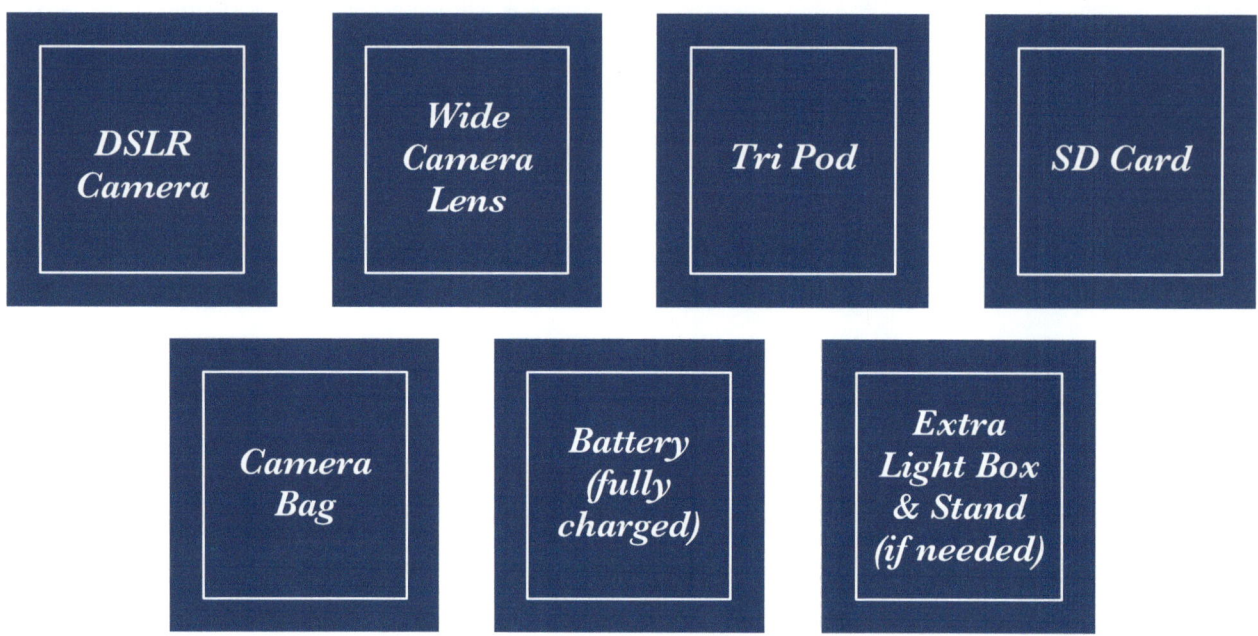

On Staging Day

After staging is complete, it is time to take the photographs. Make sure to pay attention to any loose cords or noticeable outlet plugs that you might not want to have in the photos.

You'll want to take photographs in the early morning or late afternoon to get optimum lighting for the pictures. Rainy or cloudy days are excellent days for photograph lighting.

Set the camera up on the trip-pod about 36"-42" from the ground. If you don't have a tripod, you might try sitting in a chair to get the correct view. This creates a visually pleasing picture.

Be sure to keep lamps off as they can be distracting and the light usually doesn't photograph well. Pictures will come out much cleaner and nicer looking with the lights out.

With the home already staged everything should be in order, but make sure there is not loose trash or anything that might be in the shot that shouldn't be there.

Don't use the flash setting on the camera unless absolutely necessary.

You'll want to take multiple pictures of the same shot so you have a lot to choose from later.

Photograph the angles of the room from each corner. If you have a long corridor, photograph this to emphasize that the space feels large or long.

Use the portrait, subject and aperture modes on the camera whichever looks best to capture some different types of images. Aperture works best for close up shots. You may need to take some practice shots to see which ones look the nicest.

Take a few close up shots if you have some pretty vignettes like coffee table images.

When shooting the exterior of the home, try to get all of the front of the house in the shot. Take multiple views of the front and back of the home but for sure one of the very front of the home.

Take pictures of all the main areas or rooms in the home. Try to get the maximum amount of the room in the shot or the best angle.

Always edit the pictures after shooting. Ensure that you collected all the necessary shots for the real estate listing: exterior, entry, living areas, bedrooms, bathrooms, etc.

If a photo is too dark it may be necessary to enhance the lighting or crop the picture as needed to get the best result in the frame. I use the editing software on my main computer, but there are others out there such as light room that have more options.

Remember better images capture more interest in your home's listing from both buyer's agents and buyers.

If you don't have a camera, consider borrowing from a friend, asking your real estate agent, or hiring a professional. Your home's online representation will be through these images and they are an important part of the image you are selling.

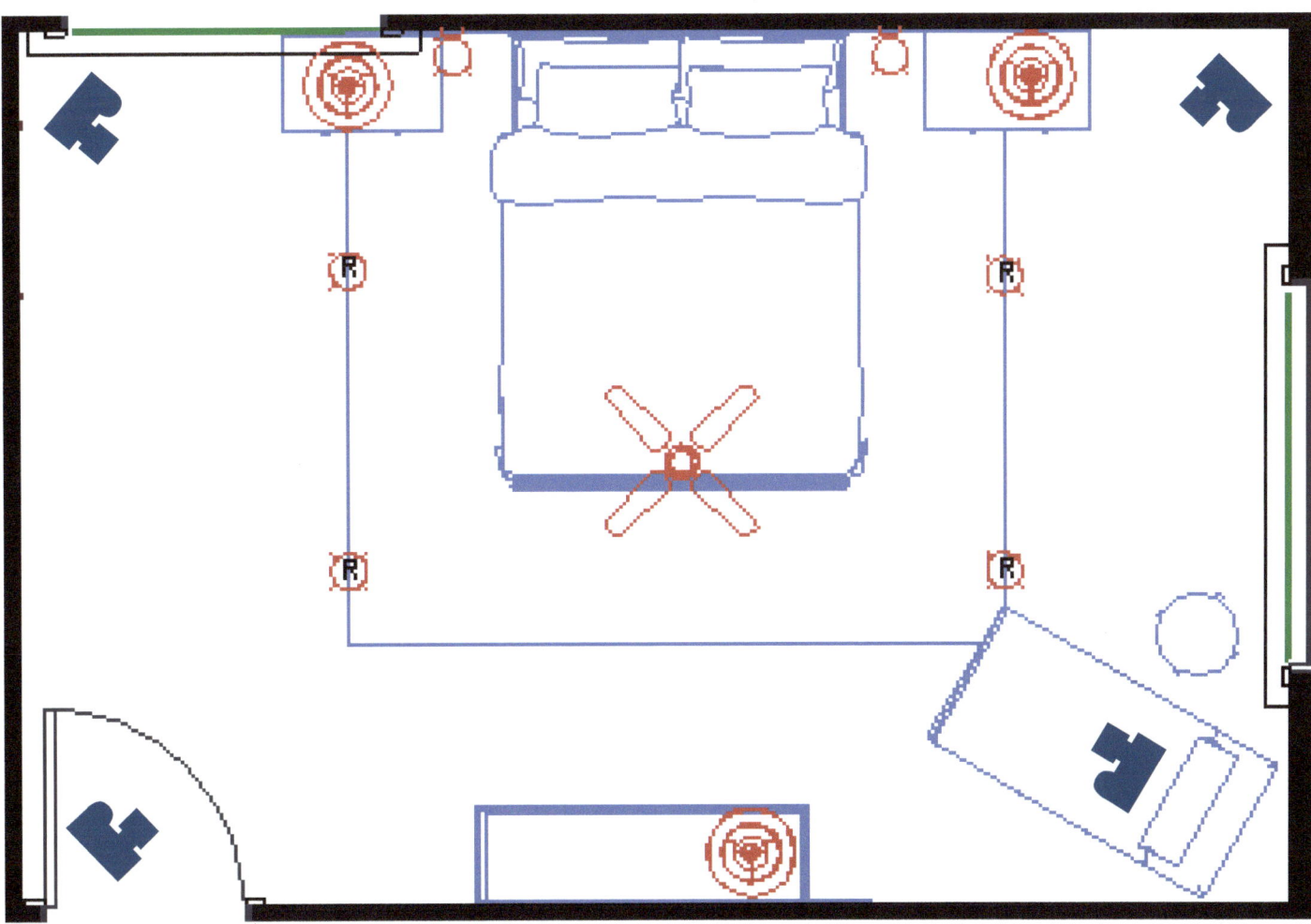

Tip: Remember to take photographs from the corners of the room in order to get the most out of your shot!

HOW TO STAGE YOUR HOME

Resources

Antique Accessories

Goodwill Industries
www.goodwill.com

Antique Trove
www.antiquetrove.com

Home Accessories

Bed Bath & Beyond
www.bedbathandbeyond.com

Dollar Tree
www.dollartree.com

Hobby Lobby
www.hobbylobby.com

Home Goods
www.homegoods.com

Ikea
www.ikea.com/us/en

Kirklands
www.kirklands.com

Kohl's
www.kohl's.com

Pier 1
www.pier1.com

Marshall's
www.marshalls.com

Target
www.target.com

Plants & Tools

Lowes
www.lowes.com

Home Depot
www.homedepot.com

Green Acres Nursery
www.idiggreenacres.com

Walmart
www.walmart.com

Furniture

Ashley Furniture
www.ashleyfurniture.com

Home Goods
www.homegoods.com

Ikea
www.ikea.com/us/en

Joss and Main
www.jossandmain.com

Kirklands
www.kirklands.com

Overstock
www.overstock.com

Pier 1
www.pier1.com

RC Willey
www.rcwilley.com

Wayfair
www.wayfair.com

World Market
www.worldmarket.com

ACKNOWLEDGMENTS

I am so very grateful first and foremost to the Lord whose presence I've always felt in my life sustaining and guiding me. I also have to thank my husband for his unconditional love and support through this process as well as my parents and children who always let me know they are my biggest fans. To my large extended family I am truly grateful to have you all in my life and to my aunt for pushing me forward with a deadline to get this done this year. A very special thanks to my daughter for her graphic design talents and coordinating the layout of this book. I also have to thank my dear friends for their listening ears, love and encouragement. Big thanks to all of my clients who allow me the privilege of working with them as we discover their style. A special thanks to the Florio family for allowing me to photograph their lovely home.

ABOUT THE AUTHOR
Christina Serrano

Christina Serrano lives in the Sacramento Valley. She is married, has three children, and a beloved golden retriever. Ten years ago, Christina received her education for design and art by training and graduating with a degree in Interior Design from American River College in Sacramento, California. In addition, she holds a degree in International Business as well as a professional diploma in Photography. Her design inspiration comes from great architecture, European design, the colors in nature, and a love of detailed patterns. What she really enjoys about design is that each new project presents an opportunity to create a custom design for her clients.

www.ingramcontent.com/pod-product-compliance
Lightning Source LLC
Chambersburg PA
CBHW041153290426
44108CB00002B/54